Who Took the Book?

Practicing the Short OO Sound

Jamal Brown

Rosen
PHONICS
READERS

Rosen
Classroom™

Mr. Hook has many books.

Mr. Hook has cookbooks.

Mr. Hook has books about crooks.

Mr. Hook has books
about football.

Mr. Hook has one
very good book.
Mr. Hook likes that book best.

Mr. Hook looks for his book.
Where is the book?

The book is missing!

Who took the book?

Mr. Hook looks everywhere.

Mr. Hook looks at his dog.
Woof! The dog took the book.

The dog thinks the book
is good, too!